MAKE FRIENDS, BREAK FRIENDS

by Peggy Burns

Illustrated by Deborah Allwright

www.raintreepublishers.co.uk
Visit our website to find out more information about **Raintree** books.

To order:
 Phone 44 (0) 1865 888112
 Send a fax to 44 (0) 1865 314091
 Visit the Raintree bookshop at **www.raintreepublishers.co.uk** to browse our
catalogue and order online.

First published in Great Britain by Raintree,
Halley Court, Jordan Hill, Oxford OX2 8EJ,
part of Harcourt Education.
Raintree is a registered trademark of Harcourt Education Ltd.

© Harcourt Education Ltd 2004
First published in paperback in 2005
The moral right of the proprietor has been asserted.

Raintree Editor: Kate Buckingham
Series Consultant: Dr Michele Elliott, Kidscape
Written by Peggy Burns
Illustrated by Deborah Allwright
Packaged by ticktock Media Ltd.
Designed by Robert Walster, BigBlu Design
Edited and project managed by Penny Worms

Printed and bound in China, by South China Printing

ISBN 1 844 43420 6 (Hardback)
08 07 06 05 04
10 9 8 7 6 5 4 3 2 1

ISBN 1 844 43425 7 (Paperback)
09 08 07 06 05
10 9 8 7 6 5 4 3 2 1

British Library Cataloguing in Publication Data
Burns, Peggy
Make Friends, Break Friends. – (Kids' Guides)
302.3'4
A full catalogue record for this book is available from the British Library.

CONTENTS

INTRODUCTION

Everybody needs friends. It is great to be able to get on well with other people and to have friends to play with. When you are unhappy about something, your friends are there to help and give you **advice**. You are there for them, too. Talking to a friend about worries helps everyone to cheer up.

Having friends makes life much more interesting, especially if they have different interests, **talents** or toys!

Making, and keeping, friends is not always easy. Some people are friendly and outgoing, others are **shy** and find it hard to make friends. Some people are easily hurt by teasing and name-calling, others are able to shrug it off and not let it bother them.

You and your friends will not always agree with each other. That is why friends sometimes **quarrel** and fall out. This book should help you when you do. And if you are feeling lonely and want to make friends, there is advice for you too.

Why can't I make friends easily?

Let's talk about...
MAKING FRIENDS

It is important to have friends. Some people enjoy being surrounded by lots of friends while others prefer to have just one or two special friends. But not everyone finds it easy to make friends. If you are **shy**, you might find it difficult to talk to people. But it's not always about being shy. Making friends is sometimes hard for people who are talkative!

You two are my best friends.

BUT WHY ME?

There can be all kinds of reasons why you might find yourself with no one to play with. Maybe the other children are not very friendly. You may have just moved or started a new school. Whatever the reason, you can do something about it.

If you want to talk to someone, it sometimes helps to think of things you could talk about. Try to find something you have in common and you could be chatting for ages. It could be the start of a great friendship.

Here are some ideas:

● talk about TV programmes or books you enjoy
● ask them to play your favourite game
● tell them you like their hairstyle
● ask them where they got their clothes.

WHY DO I FEEL LIKE THIS?

Having no friends can make anyone feel left out and lonely. Try not to look too miserable. If you look happy and friendly, it is easier for other people to talk to you.

LOOK AT IT ANOTHER WAY

It is easy to **resent** it when other people don't talk to you or leave you out of their games. But if you are shy and quiet, they may hardly know you are there. Don't wait for others to smile at you, smile at them first.

Let's talk about...

DIFFERENT PERSONALITIES

Everyone in the world is different. People come in all shapes and sizes and colours, and they all have different **personalities**. People can be cheerful or moody, good-natured or bad-tempered, selfish or generous. They have ideas, **opinions** and feelings of their own. You can learn a lot by listening to other people, but however hard you try, you are not likely to get on well with everybody.

BUT WHY ME?

If someone is being unkind to you, you have every right to feel angry or upset. But people have their own reasons for arguing or sulking. It helps to know why friends act as they do.

WHY DO I FEEL LIKE THIS?

One minute you are playing happily together, the next, your friend is in a bad mood. It is all very confusing! Perhaps you are left wondering whether you have said or done something to upset your friend. Or you might simply feel angry or worried.

Everyone has bad times when they feel unhappy.
You might have friends who are pleasant and happy for much of the time, but when things don't go their way they say nasty things, or go into a sulk and refuse to talk to you. Being ignored is just as horrid as being shouted at.

Here are some things you can do:
- talk to your friend
- try to understand why they act the way they do
- explain how hurt and upset you get.

LOOK AT IT ANOTHER WAY

Perhaps your friend has not stopped to think how they make you feel.
Getting mad might just be a **bad habit**, and bad habits can be broken.

Let's talk about...

FALLING OUT

When you are mad at someone it is easy to let your feelings take over. You start shouting, your friend shouts back, and in the heat of the moment you both say things you don't mean. Before you know it, you've fallen out. Arguments often start when you and your friend are kidding around and teasing each other. Sometimes teasing can get out of hand. One of you says something hurtful and suddenly it is not fun any more.

BUT WHY ME?

Teasing can start for all sorts of reasons. Maybe because you are tall or short, or because you are **shy** or loud. It helps to know why a friend is being nasty to you, so ask them and tell them how you feel.

Most of the time teasing is just friends having fun together. But teasing can sometimes turn nasty. If you don't enjoy your friend's teasing, here are some things you can do:

- tell them how you feel
- if it happens again, firmly tell them to stop it
- don't bottle it up if you're miserable – tell someone.

WHY DO I FEEL LIKE THIS?

Sometimes the things your friends say make you feel silly or stupid, especially when others are listening. Being treated this way makes you miserable, and it is not your fault!

LOOK AT IT ANOTHER WAY

There are always reasons why people say hurtful things. Your friend could just be **thoughtless** and not realize that he or she is hurting your feelings. But there are people who enjoy hurting others. Sometimes it is because they themselves are being picked on.

True stories

BOSSY BOOTS

Hi there. I'm Lewis, and I'm going to be a football
player one day! At school I play with my friends
every break. Some of them are pretty good –
and some aren't. For instance, Jack likes to play,
but he misses every ball.

He's hopeless!

Yesterday Jack wanted to play,
so I told him he was no good and
that he'd spoil the game. Waseem
stuck up for him. He said it wasn't
just my game. So I walked off and
let them get on with it.

Now I am standing on the sidelines watching.
I thought they would have a bad game
without me, but they're not. They're even
having a laugh. I don't know what to do.

BOSSY BOOTS Talking it through

It helps to talk to someone...

A TEACHER

Mr Graham – Lewis's teacher – comes over. He says that if Lewis wants to play for England one day he needs to learn to be part of a team. He cannot always make himself the captain.

A FRIEND

Waseem tells Lewis that he should not tell people they are no good, he should help them. Jack looked hurt and upset when Lewis told him he could not join in. How is Jack going to improve if he cannot play?

A PARENT

Lewis's mum says she is proud he is so good at football and that he is a natural leader. Maybe one day he will captain the England team. But good leaders are not bossy and he needs to learn that.

FORWARD STEPS

● LISTEN

Take notice of good advice (even when people tell you things you don't like to hear).

● ENCOURAGE OTHERS

Be a good team player – allow others to learn.

I didn't enjoy watching my friends play football without me, and I realized how Jack must have felt. It's horrible being left out. I talked things over with a few people; my mum seems to think I'm a bit bossy. (Maybe she's right!)

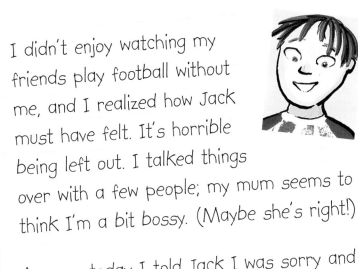

Anyway, today I told Jack I was sorry and we all played together. Jack's really keen and asked me to show him how to trap the ball. Waseem was right; I can help Jack improve.

I decided that from now on I'm going to be a real team player instead of always wanting to be the boss.

True stories

SHE LOOKS DIFFERENT

My name's Aaliah, and I go to Church Street Primary School. When we went back after the holidays Maura, a new girl, was sitting next to me. The first thing I noticed was that Maura's face was all patchy and shiny and scarred. I heard some people behind us whispering about her.

What's with the new girl, Aaliah?

Gosh, look at her face.

It looks really freaky!

Maura saw me looking at her, and she gave me a nasty look before turning her head away. I thought, well if she doesn't want to be friendly, that's fine by me! I didn't talk to her all day, even though Mrs Johnson had asked me to be nice to her.

But at playtime the next day, some people in my class started to tease Maura and say nasty things. I feel really bad for not being nice yesterday and now I feel sorry for her. I don't know what to do?

SHE LOOKS DIFFERENT

Talking it through

It helps to talk to someone...

A BIG SISTER

Her sister is sad when Aaliah tells her about Maura's scarred face. She says, 'You should try to forget the way Maura looks. It's what people are like inside that really matters.'

A TEACHER

Mrs Johnson says that nobody deserves to be teased or bullied because they look different. But she is glad that Aaliah can see that for herself. Now she could really help Maura to settle in.

A GRANDPARENT

Aaliah's gran says she should try to understand how Maura feels when people stare at her. No wonder Maura had turned away and seemed unfriendly. She probably just wants to be treated like anyone else.

FORWARD STEPS

- **TALK**

Take the trouble to find out what people are really like.

- **UNDERSTAND**

It is what a person is like on the inside that matters.

The next day, I smiled at Maura and said 'hello'. At break we started to talk. She told me that she had been burnt in a house fire and the burns had made scars that will never go away.

She said she used to be quite pretty. She's had **operations** on her face, but the doctors won't be able to make her look like she used to. I felt bad when I remembered how I'd ignored her. I said sorry because I just hadn't understood.

Maura said it was all right. She even shared her home-made biscuits with me. And the next day I told my friends about it so that they would begin to see how nice she is. Now we're all friends and don't even notice her burns!

I LIED

Hi, I'm Keeley. I did a silly thing recently, and now I feel **embarrassed** even thinking about it. I think it happened because nobody ever seemed to notice me any more.

My mum and stepdad Steve are expecting a baby, and that is all they talk about. Cots, nappies, car seats, and whether to paint the baby's room pink or blue.

You'd think I was invisible.

Even at school I'm just one of a crowd – no-one special. So one day I told my best friend Bridget that my mum had been rushed to hospital, seriously ill. Before long everybody was fussing over me. All my friends felt sorry for me. It felt good to be noticed for once!

We heard about your mum...

Are you okay?

And then Bridget saw me and Mum at the supermarket, and she knew I'd been telling lies. I feel awful and I don't know what to do.

I LIED — Talking it through

It helps to talk to someone...

A STEPPARENT

Keeley's stepdad says he is sorry for being so **pre-occupied** with the baby and he is pleased that she has told him how she feels. He promises to start taking her swimming again at weekends, like he always used to.

A PARENT

Mum reminds Keeley that she loves her very much and the baby will never take her place. She says she can understand why Keeley wants attention, but it is never good to lie to friends. She suggests Keeley tell the truth.

A FRIEND

Bridget is a bit cross about it because she and Keeley are best friends. She says that Keeley should have told her how she was feeling, and now she should tell everyone that she is sorry.

FORWARD STEPS

- **BE CONFIDENT**

Value yourself for the special person you are.

- **TELL THE TRUTH**

If you have made up stories that aren't true, talk to your friends and tell them why. Don't forget to say 'sorry'!

I was **ashamed** of making up that silly story, so I took Bridget's advice and told everyone in my class that I was really sorry for telling lies. When I explained why it had happened, they were all right about it.

Mum and Steve **apologized**. They said they'd been so excited about the baby, they hadn't thought that I might be feeling left out. We all went swimming on Saturday and then had burgers and ice cream at Pat's Pantry. After that they bought me a great new top and they let me choose the colour for the baby's room.

So everything turned out okay. But I have decided that I'm never going to tell lies to my friends again. It's not worth it!

True stories

I WISH THEY'D STOP

Hi there. My name is Kessar. That is my proper name anyway. Because I am a bit overweight my mates Charles and John call me Tubs. I know they are only teasing. They don't mean to be nasty, but it sometimes makes me feel fat and ugly.

I don't like them calling me Tubs. I wish they'd stop.

We all belong to a swimming club at the local pool. I love swimming, but wearing trunks makes them tease me even more. A few weeks ago I jumped in off the top board and made huge waves that swamped everybody. My mates didn't say much, they just laughed – but I knew exactly what they were thinking.

I've seen whales make smaller splashes!

Hee, hee. Nice one, Tubs.

I've decided not to go swimming any more. At least, not until I get a bit slimmer. (I am trying!)

I WISH THEY'D STOP

Talking it through

It helps to talk to someone...

A CLUB LEADER

Mr Walker advises Kessar to tell his mates how he feels. He reminds Kessar that swimming is a good way to exercise, and will help him to keep fit and lose weight.

A PARENT

Kessar's dad tells him that everyone at the pool is enjoying themselves too much to worry about how Kessar looks. He says the only thing Kessar should stop is having a burger and fries on his way home!

A FRIEND

Charles says he had no idea how Kessar was feeling. He tells Kessar that he would really miss him at the club. He says Kessar is a good swimmer and he shouldn't quit because of a silly name.

FORWARD STEPS

• VALUE YOURSELF

You're important – just as you are.

• HAVE FUN

But make sure that your friends are having fun too. It's never right to call people names or make fun of them *because of the way they look*.

Charles was really surprised when I told him how I felt, and he told John. They said it was just a nickname, and they hadn't realized it upset me. They promised to stop calling me Tubs. John said the swimming club wasn't the same without me, and asked me to go back.

I took my friends' **advice** and started going to the club again. These days I'm trying to forget about my size and focus on being a better swimmer. And Mr Walker's right: people who want to lose weight need exercise, and swimming is exercising and having fun at the same time!

Charles and John did stop calling me Tubs. I know now that good friends care about each other, and try not to hurt their mates' feelings.

Quiz

WHAT WOULD YOU DO?

1. What would you do if, like Lewis, people noticed that
you always wanted to be in charge, and called you Bossy Boots?
a)   Tell them firmly to mind their own business.
b)   Let them play without you to teach them a lesson.
c)   Tell a teacher that your friends are picking on you.
d)   Stop making all the decisions and give other people a chance to lead.

2. What would you do if, like Aaliah, you met someone who looked different?
a)   Ask what's wrong with them.
b)   Treat them as you would anyone else.
c)   Sympathize with them and say how sorry you were.
d)   Don't talk to them because they might not be a nice person.

3. What would you do if, like Keeley, you were tempted to make people believe
stories about yourself that weren't true?
a)   Tell them if you want to because making up stories isn't like telling real lies.
b)   Not worry about it because everyone tells lies anyway.
c)   Think of your own good points and decide that you don't need to tell lies
      about yourself.
d)   Decide that it's okay to tell lies as long as you don't get caught out.

4. What would you do if, like Kessar, you didn't like the way your friends teased you?

a) Ignore it because they might fall out with you if you tell them how you feel.

b) Start teasing them too, and see how they like it.

c) Take no notice – it's okay for friends to tease each other.

d) Tell them. Ask your friends to consider your feelings, because it hurts when they call you names, even in fun.

Answers

1. a) Remember that your friends also need to learn how to be leaders!

2. b) People who look different in some way – perhaps having scars or a birthmark – are just the same as anyone else.

3. c) You don't need to make up stories about yourself. Telling lies to your friends could make them angry or distrust you.

4. d) Always tell people how you feel. If you are hurt by the unkind things people say, that's not teasing, it's bullying – and bullying is always wrong.

Glossary

advice

when someone helps you to decide what to do or say

apologized

said 'sorry'

ashamed

Knowing that you have done something wrong and feeling bad about it

bad habit

something bad you do all the time without thinking about it

embarrassed

when you feel awkward and your face goes red

operations

something done by doctors in hospitals to repair damage done to a person's body, or to try to stop a bad disease and make a person better

opinions

things that you believe in or feel strongly about

personalities

the way you think and behave that makes you different from other people

pre-occupied

distracted and not concentrating on something

quarrel

argument or disagreement

resent

feeling bitter and angry over something you feel is unfair

shy

not confident; if you are shy you find it difficult to talk to other people

talents

things you do well, such as football, drawing or swimming

thoughtless

not thinking about whether things you do or say will affect or hurt people or damage something

Find out more

USEFUL BOOKS

Alfie Gives a Hand by Shirley Hughes
Alfie helps a shy girl at a party.

Frog and Toad are Friends by Arnold Lobel
Five stories about best friends.

Lucy's Quarrel by Jennifer Northway
Saying sorry can be difficult.

Rainbow Fish and Rainbow Fish to the Rescue by M. Pfister
Two books about sharing and making people feel left out.

Something Else by Kathryn Cave
An outsider finds friends despite being different from everyone else.

The Gotcha Smile by R. P. Mitchell
Clarine learns that a smile helps to make friends.

USEFUL WEBSITES

www.bbc.co.uk/cbbc/yourlife
A fun site about growing up, including how to deal with bullies.

www.pbskids.org
Stories for three to seven year olds and resources for parents on staying safe and feeling good about school and friends.

www.kidshealth.org
Information for parents and children on feelings and how to deal with them.

www.kidshelp.com.au
A general helpline for children.

USEFUL CONTACTS

Childline
Freepost IIII, London NI OBR
Helpline: 0800 IIII
www.childline.org.uk

For those children who need to talk to someone outside of their families.

Kidscape
2 Grosvenor Gardens, London, SWIW 0DH
Helpline: 08451 205204
www.kidscape.org.uk
Helps children being bullied or hurt by others.

Index